D0791968

Team Spirit

THE NEW YORK YANKEES

BY

MARK STEWART

Content Consultant
James L. Gates, Jr.
Library Director
National Baseball Hall of Fame and Museum

NORWOOD HOUSE PRESS
CHICAGO, ILLINOIS

Norwood House Press
P.O. Box 316598
Chicago, Illinois 60631

For information regarding Norwood House Press, please visit our website at:
www.norwoodhousepress.com or call 866-565-2900.

All photos courtesy AP/Wide World Photos, Inc. except the following:
Author's collection (6, 7 bottom, 14, 16, 17, 34 top); John Klein (13, 22, 23, 35 & & 43);
TCMA (18 & 19); Goudey Gum Company (20 & 34 right); Dexter Press (21);
Famous Publications (27); Photofest (28); GRP Records (29); Sweet Caporal (34 left); Topps, Inc (35).
Special thanks to Topps, Inc.

Editor: Mike Kennedy
Designer: Ron Jaffe
Consulting Editor: Steve Krasner
Project Management: Black Book Partners, LLC.

Special thanks to: David Sperry and Nancy Volkman.

Library of Congress Cataloging-in-Publication Data

Stewart, Mark.
  The New York Yankees / by Mark Stewart ; with content consultant James
L. Gates,Jr.
     p. cm. -- (Team spirit)
  Summary: "Presents the history, accomplishments and key personalities of
the New York Yankees baseball team. Includes timelines,quotes,maps,glossary
and websites"--Provided by publisher. Includes bibliographical references
and index.
  ISBN-13: 978-1-59953-003-1 (library edition : alk. paper)
  ISBN-10: 1-59953-003-1 (library edition : alk. paper) 1. New York
Yankees (Baseball team)--History--Juvenile literature. I. Gates,Jr.,James L.
II. Title. III. Series.
  GV875.N4.S74 2006
  796.357'64097471--dc22
                                                      2005033117

Manufactured in the United States of America.

COVER PHOTO: The New York Yankees jump for joy after winning the 2000 World Series.

Table of Contents

SPORTS WORDS & VOCABULARY WORDS: In this book, you will find many words that are new to you. You may also see familiar words used in new ways. The glossary on page 46 gives the meanings of baseball words, as well as "everyday" words that have special baseball meanings. These words appear in **bold type** throughout the book. The glossary on page 47 gives the meanings of vocabulary words that are not related to baseball. They appear in ***bold italic type*** throughout the book.

Meet the Yankees

Every player begins the season hoping he will be lucky enough to make it to the **World Series**. Imagine how it would feel to play for a team whose fans not only expect you to reach the World Series every year, but also win it! That is what it means to be a New York Yankee.

The Yankees won the **American League (A.L.) pennant** 39 times between 1921 and 2005, and went on to win the World Series 26 times—more than any other team. What does it take to play for a team that will not accept anything less than a championship? Being good is not always enough. You must be willing to do whatever the team asks of you, and you must be totally *devoted* to your teammates. When people talk about the Yankees *tradition*, this is what they are talking about.

This book tells the story of the Yankees. They are a baseball team with fans all over the country, and all over the world. They may be famous for their **Hall of Fame** hitters and pitchers, but the secret of their success is that every player makes an important contribution.

Alex Rodriguez hugs Gary Sheffield after a Yankee victory, while Hideki Matsui looks on.

5

Way Back When

When the Yankees played their first season, they were not called the Yankees. They were not even playing in New York. The team began life as the Baltimore Orioles! They were one of eight teams that made up the original A.L. in 1901. The team moved to New York City in 1903 and played their games in Manhattan's Hilltop Park. They called themselves the Highlanders. In 1913, the team changed its name to Yankees.

For many years, the Yankees were New York's "other" team. The New York Giants had some of the game's brightest stars, and they were managed by a powerful man named John McGraw. In 1920, the city's baseball picture began to change. The Yankees got a young power hitter from the Boston Red Sox. His name was Babe Ruth, and in his first year with the Yankees he hit 54 home runs—25 more than anyone else in history!

ABOVE: A cheerleader warms up the crowd at Hilltop Park.
TOP RIGHT: Babe Ruth and Lou Gehrig with manager Miller Huggins.
BOTTOM RIGHT: Babe Ruth had his own board game during the 1920s.

Fans poured into the ballpark to see Ruth hit home runs. The Yankees used the money they made to build a brand new ball park in 1923, Yankee Stadium. That fall, they beat the Giants in the World Series. The Yankees surrounded Ruth with other good hitters, including Lou Gehrig, Bob Meusel, Tony Lazzeri, Earle Combs—all of whom are in the Hall of Fame.

From the 1920s to the 1960s, the Yankees were the most successful team in sports. They won the A.L. pennant 29 times during this period, and were World Series champions 20 times. Some legendary hitters played for these great teams. Besides Ruth and Gehrig, the Yankee **lineup** included Joe DiMaggio, Bill Dickey, Yogi Berra, Roger Maris, and Mickey Mantle. The team also had wonderful pitchers, including Waite Hoyt, Red Ruffing, Lefty Gomez, Allie Reynolds, and Whitey Ford.

In the 1960s and early 1970s, the Yankees were owned by the CBS television network. During that time the Yankees sank in the **standings**. Things turned around when George Steinbrenner became the owner in 1973. Steinbrenner loved to win, and he decided to spend whatever it took to bring back the glory years. Led by Thurman Munson, Reggie Jackson, and Ron Guidry, the Yankees won four pennants between 1976 and 1981. The Yankee tradition of winning baseball was reborn, and it continues to this day.

LEFT: Yogi Berra and Mickey Mantle
pose together before a 1956 game at Yankee Stadium.
TOP: Thurman Munson, the captain of the Yankees during the 1970s.

9

The Team Today

Since the mid 1990s, the Yankees have been the most successful team in baseball. Their winning *strategy* has been "strength up the middle"—good, smart players at catcher, shortstop, second base, and center field. These players have included Derek Jeter, Bernie Williams, and Jorge Posada, who were on six World Series teams together between 1996 and 2003.

All three of these stars learned the game in the Yankees' **minor league** system. Like all of the team's young **prospects**, they were taught good **fundamentals**, and learned that they were part of a winning tradition. When minor leaguers are called up to join the Yankees, they are ready to compete at the highest level.

This helps the Yankees when they look for new players. The team always has a chance to win a championship, so even the game's best players are anxious to play for New York. The Yankees are baseball's richest ball club. they can afford to hire the best players. Their challenge is to find great players who are willing to do whatever it takes to be a part of a winning team.

Derek Jeter congratulates Jorge Posada after a home run.

Home Turf

When Yankee Stadium opened in 1923, it was the most fantastic sports stadium in America. Some called it a "*cathedral* of baseball." The stadium was built to help left-handed **sluggers**. The right field wall was very close to home plate. The left field wall was very far away, which made it difficult for right-handers to hit home runs. Not surprisingly, most of the team's great hitters have been left-handed.

Yankee Stadium was modernized in the 1970s. The shape of the field is the same, but the difference between right field and left field is not as great as it once was. A group of monuments honoring the team's great players is now located beyond the left field wall. Before the 1970s, these monuments were actually on the field.

YANKEE STADIUM BY THE NUMBERS

- *Yankee Stadium has 57,545 seats.*
- *The distance from home plate to the left field foul pole is 318 feet.*
- *The distance from home plate to the center field wall is 408 feet.*
- *The distance from home plate to the right field foul pole is 314 feet.*
- *In 2005, the team unveiled plans for a new Yankee Stadium, which will be located across the street.*

Some of baseball's greatest moments have taken place at Yankee Stadium.

Dressed for Success

The Yankees' uniform may be the most famous in baseball. The team has been wearing dark blue *pinstripes* since 1912. They have used the "NY" *logo* on their hats since 1909. A larger version of this logo has been used on the uniform top since 1936. Over the next 70 years, New York's uniform changed very little.

The Yankees wear their pinstripes at home, and use a grey uniform with "New York" across the chest on the road. They have worn solid blue stirrup socks for more than 90 years. The Yankees' "NY" can be found on hats and shorts in almost every country in the world. When the team signed Japanese star Hideki Matsui in 2003, stores in Tokyo sold out of Yankees merchandise in a few days.

Joe DiMaggio wears the classic Yankee pinstripes.

The baseball uniform has not changed much since the Yankees began playing. It has four main parts:

- a cap or batting helmet with a sun visor;
- a top with a player's number on the back;
- pants that reach down between the ankle and the knee;
- stirrup-style socks.

The uniform top sometimes has a player's name on the back. The team's name, city, or logo is usually on the front. Baseball teams wear light-colored uniforms when they play at home, and darker styles when they play on the road.

For more than 100 years, baseball uniforms were made of wool *flannel* and were very baggy. This helped the sweat *evaporate* and gave players the freedom to move around. Today's uniforms are made of *synthetic* fabrics that stretch with players and keep them dry and cool.

Scott Brosius, with his pants worn to show his stirrup socks, celebrates a home run in the 2001 World Series.

We Won!

O ver the past 100 years, Yankees fans have gotten used to winning. So many champions have worn pinstripes that fans often argue about which club was the best ever. The Yankees of the 1920s won six pennants in eight years. They were led by Babe Ruth, who changed the way baseball was played with his incredible slugging. Along with Ruth, Lou Gehrig, Bob Meusel, Earle Combs, and Tony Lazzeri supplied the hitting for these great teams. Waite Hoyt, Herb Pennock, and Bob Shawkey took care of the pitching. The Yankees won the World Series in 1923, 1927, and 1928.

Bob Meusel, Babe Ruth, and Earle Combs—together they formed one of the greatest outfields of all time.

The Yankees teams of the 1930s and early 1940s were even more successful. They won eight pennants in 12 years, and were the best team in baseball. These teams had hitting stars like Gehrig, and Bill Dickey, Charlie Keller, Joe Gordon, and Tommy Henrich.

The 1939 Yankees pose with New York schoolchildren.

Their pitching was led by Red Ruffing, Lefty Gomez, Johnny Murphy, and Spud Chandler. The biggest star of this period was Joe DiMaggio, who joined the team in 1936. In 1941, he set a record by reaching base on a hit in 56 games in a row. The Yankees won the World Series seven times between 1932 and 1943, including four in a row between 1936 and 1939.

In the years after World War II, the Yankees were the best team in baseball again. Between 1947 and 1964, they won the pennant in all but three seasons. The team's pitching staff was excellent. It was led by Allie Reynolds, Vic Raschi, Joe Page, Eddie Lopat, Whitey Ford, and Bob Turley. These teams also starred great hitters, including Bobby Richardson, Yogi Berra, Phil Rizzuto, Billy Martin,

Bill Skowron, Elston Howard, Roger Maris, and Mickey Mantle. During this era, the Yankees won the World Series 10 times—including five in a row from 1949 to 1953. Their most dramatic championship came in 1958, when they defeated the Milwaukee Braves after trailing three games to one.

The Yankees returned to power again in the 1970s. They won the pennant four times between 1976 and 1981, and won the World Series in 1977 and 1978. The stars of these teams included Thurman Munson, Graig Nettles, Reggie Jackson, Mickey Rivers, Lou Piniella, Willie Randolph, Ron Guidry, and Goose Gossage.

Yet another group of stars led the Yankees to the top of baseball starting in the mid 1990s. Derek Jeter, Bernie Williams, Paul O'Neill, Jorge Posada, Andy Pettitte, and Mariano Rivera formed the heart of a team that won the pennant six times between 1996 and 2003. The Yankees won the World Series in 1996 and three times in a row from 1998 to 2000.

ABOVE: Mickey Mantle (top) and Roger Maris pose for trading cards with Yankee Stadium's famous upper deck facade in the background.
RIGHT: The Yankees celebrate their victory in the 1999 World Series.

Go-To Guys

To be a true star in baseball, you need more than a quick bat and a strong arm. You have to be a "go-to guy"—someone the manager wants on the pitcher's mound or in the batter's box when it matters most. Yankees fans have had a lot to cheer about over the years, including these great stars…

THE PIONEERS

BABE RUTH   Outfielder

• BORN: 2/6/1895 • DIED: 8/16/1948 • PLAYED FOR TEAM: 1920 TO 1934

Babe Ruth was the greatest power hitter in history. He slugged 60 home runs in 1927, and 714 in his career.

LOU GEHRIG   First Baseman

• BORN: 6/19/1903 • DIED: 6/2/1941
• PLAYED FOR TEAM: 1923 TO 1939

Lou Gehrig was a **line drive** machine, spraying hits all over the field—including 493 home runs. He was tough, too. Gehrig once played 2,130 games in a row.

ABOVE: Lou Gehrig **RIGHT**: Whitey Ford

JOE DiMAGGIO   Outfielder

• BORN: 11/25/1914   • DIED: 3/8/1999   • PLAYED FOR TEAM: 1936 TO 1951

Joe DiMaggio was the best **all-around** player who ever wore a Yankee uniform. He was the league's best hitter, baserunner and fielder during the 1930s.

YOGI BERRA   Catcher

• BORN: 5/12/1925   • PLAYED FOR TEAM: 1946 TO 1963

Yogi Berra was one of baseball's greatest **clutch hitters**. If the Yankees needed a hit late in a game, there was no one they would rather send to bat.

MICKEY MANTLE   Outfielder

• BORN: 10/20/1931   • DIED: 8/13/1995   • PLAYED FOR TEAM: 1951 TO 1968

Mickey Mantle was the most powerful **switch-hitter** in history. He hit more long home runs than anyone during the 1950s and 1960s.

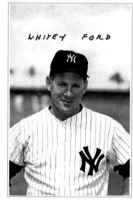

WHITEY FORD   Pitcher

• BORN: 10/21/1928   • PLAYED FOR TEAM: 1950 TO 1967

The Yankees had a lot of big, hard-throwing pitchers over the years, but their best pitcher was little Whitey Ford.

ROGER MARIS   Outfielder

• BORN: 9/10/1934   • DIED: 12/14/1985   • PLAYED FOR TEAM: 1960 TO 1966

Roger Maris broke Babe Ruth's record when he hit 61 home runs in 1961. Most fans thought of Maris as a slugger, but he was an excellent fielder and baserunner, too.

THURMAN MUNSON   Catcher

• BORN: 6/7/1947 • DIED: 8/2/1979 • PLAYED FOR TEAM: 1969 TO 1979

Thurman Munson was the leader of the Yankees during the 1970s. He won the **Most Valuable Player (MVP)** Award in 1976. Munson was killed in a plane crash three years later.

REGGIE JACKSON   Outfielder

• BORN: 5/18/1946 • PLAYED FOR TEAM: 1977 TO 1981

Reggie Jackson loved to be in the spotlight. He played his best in the **postseason**, and earned the nickname "Mr. October." Jackson hit 12 home runs in 34 playoff and World Series games as a Yankee.

DON MATTINGLY   First Baseman

• BORN: 4/20/1961

• PLAYED FOR TEAM: 1982 TO 1995

Don Mattingly was the team's best player from the mid 1980s to the mid 1990s. The fans called him "Donnie Baseball" because he loved the game so much. A bad back forced Mattingly to retire before he had a chance to win a championship.

BERNIE WILLIAMS   Outfielder

• BORN: 9/13/1968 • FIRST YEAR WITH TEAM: 1991

Bernie Williams played center field for the Yankees longer than Joe DiMaggio and Mickey Mantle. He batted over .300 eight times in a row.

ANDY PETTITTE   Pitcher

- BORN: 6/15/1972   • PLAYED FOR TEAM: 1995 TO 2003

Andy Pettitte was one of the best "big-game" pitcher in the team's history. When the Yankees were desperate for a victory, he was the man teammates loved to see on the mound.

MARIANO RIVERA   Pitcher

- BORN: 11/29/1969

- FIRST YEAR WITH TEAM: 1995

Mariano Rivera became baseball's best relief pitcher with the Yankees. He set the team record for **saves** with 50 in 2001.

DEREK JETER   Shortstop

- BORN: 6/26/1974   • FIRST YEAR WITH TEAM: 1995

Derek Jeter became one of the best all-around players the Yankees ever had. He led the league in hits in 1999, and won **Gold Glove** awards in 2004 and 2005.

ALEX RODRIGUEZ   Third Base

- BORN: 7/27/1975   • FIRST YEAR WITH TEAM: 2004

Alex Rodriguez spent his early childhood right across the East River from Yankee Stadium. When he had a chance to join the team in 2004, the Gold Glove shortstop agreed to switch positions just so he could wear the Yankee uniform.

LEFT: Don Mattingly   **ABOVE**: Mariano Rivera

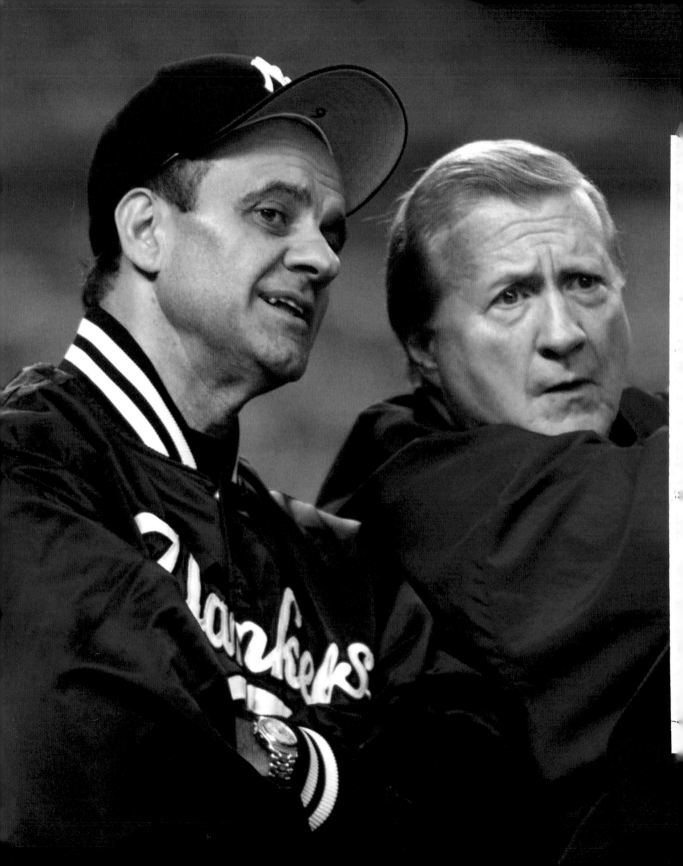

On the Sidelines

Winning championships takes talented players. It also helps to have a manager who knows how to succeed. The Yankees have had more Hall of Famers manage them than any team in baseball. The list includes Clark Griffith, Frank Chance, Miller Huggins, Joe McCarthy, Bucky Harris, Casey Stengel, Bob Lemon, and Yogi Berra.

Huggins managed the great teams of the 1920s. He had his hands full with Babe Ruth, who was wild and *unpredictable* off the field. McCarthy managed the Yankees during the 1930s. He was an excellent teacher and rarely made a mistake in strategy. Stengel was New York's leader during the 1950s. He loved to "platoon" players, using two men with different skills at the same position.

New York's two most beloved managers were Billy Martin and Joe Torre. Martin managed the team four different times in the 1970s and 1980s. He was famous for his arguments with owner George Steinbrenner. In 1996, Steinbrenner hired Torre to run the team. He won four World Series between 1996 and 2000. Torre was a very good player and a great manager. He may well be voted into the Hall of Fame some day.

Joe Torre and George Steinbrenner watch the Yankees during warm-ups.

One Great Day

The best a pitcher can do in a nine-inning game is to face 27 batters and get 27 outs. This is called a "perfect game." In the last 100 years, fewer than a dozen pitchers have thrown a perfect game. When Don Larsen delivered the first pitch in Game Five of the 1956 World Series, no one in Yankee Stadium thought they would be *witnessing* perfection that day.

Larsen was not New York's best pitcher. He had a good fastball, but the Brooklyn Dodgers had already hit him hard in Game Two. They could hardly wait to face him a second time. To their surprise, Larsen got them to ground out, fly out, or strike out inning after inning. Not a single Dodger made it to first base. The closest thing to a hit was a line drive by Gil Hodges to left-center field, which Mickey Mantle caught after a long run.

In the ninth inning, with the Yankees winning 2–0, Larsen took a deep breath and went to work. The first batter, Carl Furillo, fouled off four pitches before flying out. The second batter, Roy Campanella, grounded out to second base. The third man up was Dale Mitchell, a

ABOVE: Don Larsen delivers a pitch against the Brooklyn Dodgers. **RIGHT**: His perfect game in the 1956 World Series was front-page news.

pinch-hitting specialist who was batting for the pitcher. Larsen got two strikes on Mitchell.

With everyone in Yankee Stadium on their feet, Larsen threw a fastball on the **outside corner** and umpire Babe Pinelli called it strike three. The game was over. Catcher Yogi Berra popped out of his crouch and jumped into Larsen's arms. No one could believe what they had just seen. As one newspaper put it the next day, "The imperfect man had pitched a perfect game."

Legend Has It

Did Babe Ruth predict his own home run in the 1932 World Series?

LEGEND HAS IT that he did. Batting against the Cubs in Wrigley Field, Ruth was being booed by the fans and *insulted* by the Chicago players. After pitcher Charlie Root threw a strike, Ruth held up one finger. When Root threw a second strike, Ruth held up two fingers. Then he pointed to center field and said something that no one could hear. Ruth hit the next pitch high into the center field **bleachers** and rounded the bases with a big smile on his face. Ruth claimed he "called" his home run. The Cubs claimed he did not. No one will ever know for sure.

Long after Babe Ruth retired, he loved to tell the story of his "called shot."

Could Joe DiMaggio have hit in more than 60 straight games?

LEGEND HAS IT that he almost did. In 1941, DiMaggio set a record with at least one hit in 56 games in a row. In the 57th game, third baseman Ken Keltner of the Cleveland Indians made two diving plays to rob DiMaggio of hits. The next day, he started another hitting streak of 16 games.

Which Yankee had the most talent off the field?

BERNIE WILLIAMS The Journey Within

LEGEND HAS IT that Bernie Williams was the most artistic Yankee. Many Yankees have had parts in movies, including Babe Ruth, Lou Gehrig, and Mickey Mantle. George Steinbrenner has acted in beer and credit card commercials. Derek Jeter once hosted the TV show "Saturday Night Live." But Williams wins for his wonderful 2003 CD *The Journey Within.* Few fans realized that he gave up a career in music for a career in baseball at the age of 16.

It Really Happened

In 1996, the Yankees began an amazing streak. They would make it to the World Series that year, and they would return five times in the next seven seasons. The player who got them started was Derek Jeter—with a "helping hand" from a young fan.

The Yankees were playing the Baltimore Orioles in the opening game of the **American League Championship Series (ALCS)**. The

Orioles needed a win at Yankee Stadium to *seize* control of the series. They were leading 4–3 in the eighth inning when Jeter— a 22-year-old **rookie**— stepped to the plate.

Armando Benitez threw Jeter a fastball and he lifted

Derek Jeter answers questions after another New York victory. His controversial home run in the 1996 playoffs was one of the biggest hits of his career.

Jeffrey Maier reaches for Derek Jeter's long drive, and Tony Tarasco comes up empty.

a high fly ball to right field. Tony Tarasco drifted back to the fence and jumped up to catch the ball. Suddenly, a hand flashed out over the wall and stopped the ball before it went into Tarasco's glove. The ball bounced into the stands for a home run to tie the game. That hand belonged to 13-year-old Jeffrey Maier.

The Orioles argued that the boy had interfered with the ball, and that Jeter should have been called out. The umpire refused to change his decision. The Yankees went on to win the game in extra innings, and they beat the **demoralized** Orioles four games to one. To this day, the name Jeffrey Maier makes Derek Jeter smile—and drives Orioles fans crazy!

Team Spirit

After the terror attacks of September 11, 2001, the people of New York were badly shaken. Many had lost friends and family. Much of their city lay in ruins. When the Yankees made it to the World Series that October, New Yorkers hoped that they would have something to cheer about.

Unfortunately, the team lost the first two games in Arizona to the Diamondbacks. They returned to Yankee Stadium a tired, beaten team. Over the next three games, however, the emotion of the crowd re-energized the Yankees.

The Yankees *trailed* the Diamondbacks late in each game. Yet each time they fought and struggled to win. Fans who live outside of New York root often against the Yankees. That fall, a lot of Americans became Yankees fans.

The Diamondbacks ended up winning the World Series, but the three unforgettable victories in New York helped raise the spirits of millions of New Yorkers. The Yankees and their fans built a special relationship during those games in Yankee Stadium. The city will never forget how the team refused to lose, and the team will never forget that the fans were with them every step of the way.

The fans at Yankee Stadium show their support during the 2001 World Series.

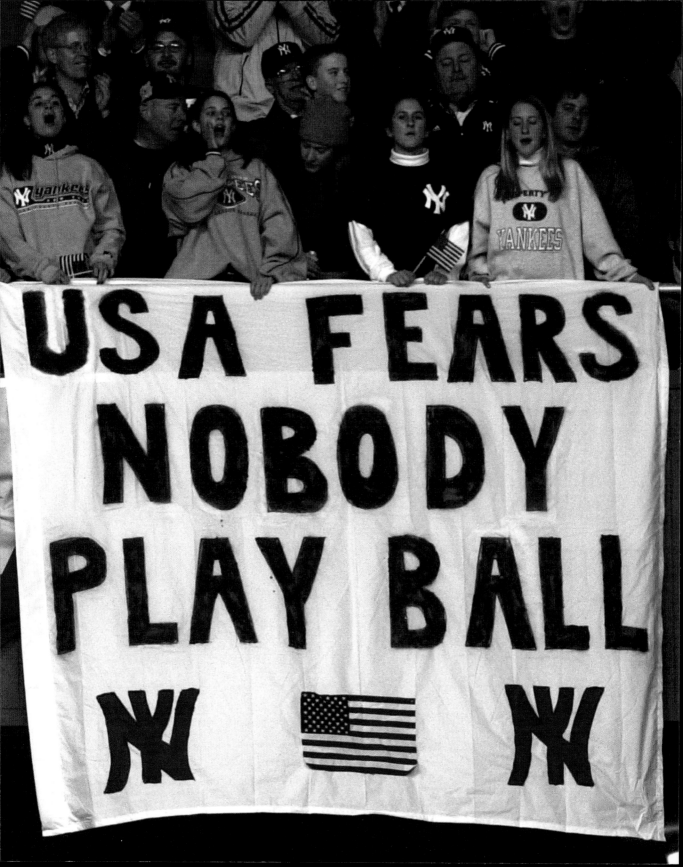

Timeline

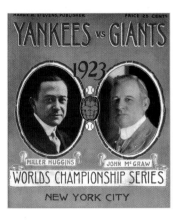

A 1923 World Series program featuring Miller Huggins and John McGraw.

1901
The team plays its first season as the Baltimore Orioles.

1913
The Highlanders become the Yankees.

1923
The Yankees win their first World Series.

1903
The team moves to New York and becomes the Highlanders.

1920
The Yankees get Babe Ruth from the Boston Red Sox.

1927
Babe Ruth hits 60 home runs in a season.

Jack Chesbro, who won 104 games for the Highlanders in their first four seasons.

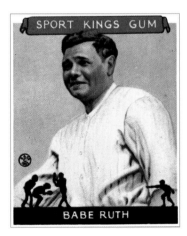

Roger
Maris

Don
Mattingly

1941
Joe DiMaggio
hits in 56
straight games.

1961
Roger Maris breaks
Ruth's record with
61 home runs.

1987
Don Mattingly hits a
home run in eight
straight games.

1953
The Yankees win
their fifth World
Series in a row.

1977
Reggie Jackson hits
three home runs in
Game Six of the
World Series.

2000
The Yankees beat the
Mets in the first all-
New York World
Series in 44 years.

Reggie
Jackson

Fun Facts

ONE-MAN SHOW

In 1920, Babe Ruth hit 54 home runs for the Yankees. No other *team* in the league hit more than 50.

SPEED DEMON

Mickey Mantle is remembered as the greatest power hitter of his time. Before he injured his knee as a rookie, he was also baseball's fastest player.

NUMBERS GAME

The Yankees were the first baseball team to "retire" famous numbers. Once a number is retired, it cannot be worn again.

YOU'RE HIRED…NO YOU'RE FIRED

Yankees owner George Steinbrenner could never decide whether he loved or hated manager Billy Martin. He fired Martin four different times. In all, Steinbrenner changed managers 19 times during the first 20 years he owned the Yankees.

RIGHT: Joe DiMaggio with his wife, Marilyn Monroe. **BELOW**: Reggie Jackson takes a bite out of his own candy bar. **LEFT**: George Steinbrenner

STAR POWER

After Joe DiMaggio retired in the 1950s, he married movie star Marilyn Monroe.

IT JUST TAKES ONE SWING

The Yankees have won the A.L. pennant with **walk-off home runs** twice. In 1976, Chris Chambliss blasted one into the seats against the Kansas City Royals. In 2003, Aaron Boone hit one out against the Boston Red Sox.

SWEET

Reggie Jackson once joked that if he played in New York, they would name a candy bar after him. In 1977, Jackson signed with the Yankees. A few months later, the REGGIE! bar was in candy stores across America.

Talking Baseball

"It's great to be young and a Yankee!"

—*Waite Hoyt, on playing baseball in New York*

"Baseball was...is...and always will be to me, the best game in the world."

—*Babe Ruth, on why he loved to play*

"There is no room in baseball for **discrimination**. It is our national pastime and a game for all."

—*Lou Gehrig, on the rule that barred African-Americans from baseball when he played*

"There is always some kid who may be seeing me for the first or last time. I owe him my best."

—*Joe DiMaggio, on why playing hard was so important to him*

Lou Gehrig and Joe DiMaggio played together for four seasons.

Alex Rodriguez follows through on a swing.

"So I'm ugly. So what? I never saw anyone hit with his face."

—Yogi Berra, on being teased about the way he looked

"One of the best things about being a Yankee is that you have guys like Whitey Ford, Phil Rizzuto, Ron Guidry, and Reggie Jackson wandering around the locker room offering you advice."

—Derek Jeter, on getting tips from great Yankees of the past

"You can never be perfect in this game.
Until you hit 1.000 and make no errors, you can always improve."

—Alex Rodriguez, on the challenge of baseball

For the Record

T he great Yankees teams and players have left their marks on the record books. These are the "best of the best"…

YANKEES AWARD WINNERS

WINNER	AWARD	YEAR	WINNER	AWARD	YEAR
Lou Gehrig	MVP	1936	Thurman Munson	Rookie of the Year	1970
Joe DiMaggio	MVP	1939			
Joe DiMaggio	MVP	1941	Thurman Munson	MVP	1976
Joe Gordon	MVP	1942	Sparky Lyle	Cy Young Award	1977
Spud Chandler	MVP	1943	Ron Guidry	Cy Young Award	1978
Joe DiMaggio	MVP	1947	Dave Righetti	Rookie of the Year	1981
Phil Rizzuto	MVP	1950	Don Mattingly	MVP	1985
Gil McDougald	Rookie of the Year[†]	1951	Buck Showalter	Manager of the Year	1994
Yogi Berra	MVP	1951	Joe Torre	Manager of the Year	1996
Bob Grim	Rookie of the Year	1954	Derek Jeter	Rookie of the Year	1996
Yogi Berra	MVP	1954	Joe Torre	Manager of the Year	1998
Yogi Berra	MVP	1955	Roger Clemens	Cy Young Award	2001
Mickey Mantle	MVP	1956	Alex Rodriguez	MVP	2005
Tony Kubek	Rookie of the Year	1957			
Mickey Mantle	MVP	1957			
Bob Turley	Cy Young Award[*]	1958			
Roger Maris	MVP	1960			
Whitey Ford	Cy Young Award	1961			
Roger Maris	MVP	1961			
Tom Tresh	Rookie of the Year	1962			
Mickey Mantle	MVP	1962			
Elston Howard	MVP	1963			
Stan Bahnsen	Rookie of the Year	1968			

*The trophy given to the league's best pitcher each year.
† An award given to the league's best first-year player.

Roger Maris, Yogi Berra and Mickey Mantle pose for the camera.

YANKEES ACHIEVEMENTS

ACHIEVEMENT	YEAR	ACHIEVEMENT	YEAR
A.L. Pennant Winner	1921	World Series Champions	1952
A.L. Pennant Winner	1922	A.L. Pennant Winner	1953
A.L. Pennant Winner	1923	World Series Champions	1953
World Series Champions	1923	A.L. Pennant Winner	1955
A.L. Pennant Winner	1926	A.L. Pennant Winner	1956
A.L. Pennant Winner	1927	World Series Champions	1956
World Series Champions	1927	A.L. Pennant Winner	1957
A.L. Pennant Winner	1928	A.L. Pennant Winner	1958
World Series Champions	1928	World Series Champions	1958
A.L. Pennant Winner	1932	A.L. Pennant Winner	1960
World Series Champions	1932	A.L. Pennant Winner	1961
A.L. Pennant Winner	1936	World Series Champions	1961
World Series Champions	1936	A.L. Pennant Winner	1962
A.L. Pennant Winner	1937	World Series Champions	1962
World Series Champions	1937	A.L. Pennant Winner	1963
A.L. Pennant Winner	1938	A.L. Pennant Winner	1964
World Series Champions	1938	A.L. Pennant Winner	1976
A.L. Pennant Winner	1939	A.L. Pennant Winner	1977
World Series Champions	1939	World Series Champions	1977
A.L. Pennant Winner	1941	A.L. Pennant Winner	1978
World Series Champions	1941	World Series Champions	1978
A.L. Pennant Winner	1942	A.L. Pennant Winner	1981
A.L. Pennant Winner	1943	A.L. Pennant Winner	1996
World Series Champions	1943	World Series Champions	1996
A.L. Pennant Winner	1947	A.L. Pennant Winner	1998
World Series Champions	1947	World Series Champions	1998
A.L. Pennant Winner	1949	A.L. Pennant Winner	1999
World Series Champions	1949	World Series Champions	1999
A.L. Pennant Winner	1950	A.L. Pennant Winner	2000
World Series Champions	1950	World Series Champions	2000
A.L. Pennant Winner	1951	A.L. Pennant Winner	2001
World Series Champions	1951	A.L. Pennant Winner	2003
A.L. Pennant Winner	1952		

Pinpoints

The history of a baseball team is made up of many smaller stories. These stories take place all over the map—not just in the city a team calls "home." Match the push-pins on these maps to the Team Facts and you will begin to see the story of the Yankees unfold!

TEAM FACTS

1 Baltimore, Maryland—*The team played here in 1901 and 1902.*

2 New York City, New York—*The team has played here since 1903.*

3 Pequannock, New Jersey—*Derek Jeter was born here.*

4 Evansville, Indiana—*Don Mattingly was born here.*

5 St. Louis, Missouri—*Yogi Berra was born here.*

6 Hibbing, Minnesota—*Roger Maris was born here.*

7 Commerce, Oklahoma—*Mickey Mantle was born here.*

8 Lafayette, Louisiana—*Ron Guidry was born here.*

9 Martinez, California—*Joe DiMaggio was born here.*

10 San Juan, Puerto Rico—*Bernie Williams was born here.*

11 Panama City, Panama—*Mariano Rivera was born here.*

12 Ishikawa, Japan—*Hideki Matsui was born here.*

Bernie Williams

Play Ball

Baseball is a game played between two teams over nine innings. Teams take one turn at bat and one turn in the field during each inning. A turn at bat ends when three outs are made. The batters on the hitting team try to reach base safely. The players on the fielding team try to prevent this from happening.

In baseball, the ball is controlled by the pitcher. The pitcher must throw the ball to the batter, who decides whether or not to swing at each pitch. If a batter swings and misses, it is a strike. If the batter lets a good pitch go by, it is also a strike. If the batter swings and the ball does not stay in fair territory (between the v-shaped lines that begin at home plate) it is called "foul," and is counted as a strike. If the pitcher throws three strikes, the batter is out. If the pitcher throws four bad pitches before that, the batter is awarded first base. This is called a base-on-balls, or "walk."

When the batter swings the bat and hits the ball, everyone springs into action. If a fielder catches a batted ball before it hits the ground, the batter is out. If a fielder scoops the ball off the ground and throws it to first base before the batter arrives, the batter is out. If the batter reaches first base safely, he is credited with a hit. A one-base hit is called a single, a two-base hit is called a double, a three-base hit is called a triple, and a four-base hit is called a home run.

Runners who reach base are only safe when they are touching one of the bases. If they are caught between the bases, the fielders can tag them with the ball and record an out.

A batter who is able to circle the bases and make it back to home plate before three outs are made is credited with a run scored. The team with the most runs after nine innings is the winner.

Anyone who has played baseball (or softball) knows that it can be a complicated game. Every player on the field has a job to do. Different players have different strengths and weaknesses. The pitchers, batters, and managers make hundreds of decisions every game. The more you play and watch baseball, the more "little things" you are likely to notice. The next time you are at a game, look for these plays:

PLAY LIST

DOUBLE PLAY—A play where the fielding team is able to make two outs on one batted ball. This usually happens when a runner is on first base, and the batter hits the ball to one of the infielders. The base runner is forced out at second base and the ball is then thrown to first base before the batter arrives.

HIT AND RUN—A play where the runner on first base sprints to second base while the pitcher is throwing the ball to the batter. When the second baseman or shortstop moves toward the base to wait for the catcher's throw, the batter tries to hit the ball to the place that the fielder has just left. If the batter swings and misses, the fielding team can tag the runner out.

INTENTIONAL WALK—A play when the pitcher throws four bad pitches on purpose, allowing the batter to walk to first base. This happens when the pitcher would much rather face the next batter—and is willing to risk putting a runner on base.

SACRIFICE BUNT—A play where the batter makes an out on purpose so that a teammate can move to the next base. On a bunt, the batter tries to "deaden" the pitch with the bat instead of swinging at it.

SHOESTRING CATCH—A play where an outfielder catches a short hit an inch or two above the ground, near the tops of his shoes. It is not easy to run as fast as you can and lower your glove without slowing down. It can be risky, too. If a fielder misses a shoestring catch, the ball might roll all the way to the fence.

Glossary

BASEBALL WORDS TO KNOW

ALL-AROUND—Good at all parts of the game.

AMERICAN LEAGUE (A.L.)—One of baseball's two major leagues. The A.L. started play in 1901. The National league N.L. started play in 1876.

AMERICAN LEAGUE CHAMPIONSHIP SERIES (ALCS)—The competition that has decided the A.L. pennant winner since 1969.

BLEACHERS—The unprotected seats located in the outfield, where fans get "bleached" by the sun.

CLUTCH HITTERS—Hitters who do well under pressure, or "in the clutch."

FUNDAMENTALS—The basic skills of baseball.

GOLD GLOVE—An award given each year to baseball's best fielders.

HALL OF FAME—The museum in Cooperstown, NY where baseball's greatest players are honored. A player voted into the Hall of Fame is sometimes called a "Hall of Famer."

LINE DRIVE—A hard hit that does not rise very far off the ground.

LINEUP—The list of players who are playing in a game.

MINOR LEAGUES—The many professional leagues that help develop players for the major leagues.

MOST VALUABLE PLAYER (MVP)—An award given each year to the league's top player; an MVP is also selected for the World Series and All-Star Game.

OUTSIDE CORNER—The area above the edge of home plate that is farthest from the batter.

PENNANT—A league championship. The term comes from the triangular flag awarded to each season's champion, beginning in the 1870s.

POSTSEASON—The games played after the regular season, including playoff and World Series games.

PROSPECTS—Young players who are expected to become stars.

ROOKIE—A player in his first season.

SAVES—A statistic relief pitchers earn when they get the final out of a close game.

SLUGGERS—Powerful hitters.

STANDINGS—A daily list of teams, starting with the team with the best record and ending with the team with the worst record.

SWITCH-HITTERS—Players who can hit from either side of home plate. Switch-hitters bat left-handed against right-handed pitchers, and bat right-handed against left-handed pitchers.

WALK-OFF HOME RUNS—Game-ending home runs hit in last half of the final inning.

WORLD SERIES—The world championship series played between the winners of the National League and American League.

OTHER WORDS TO KNOW

CATHEDRAL—A large church.

DEMORALIZED—Having lost spirit or morale.

DEVOTED—Loyal.

DISCRIMINATION—The act of treating someone badly because of who they are or how they look.

EVAPORATE—Disappear, or turn into a vapor.

FLANNEL—A soft wool or cotton material.

INSULTED—Spoke to someone in a way that hurts their feelings.

LOGO—A symbol or design that represents a company or team.

PINSTRIPES—Thin stripes.

SEIZE—To capture or control.

STRATEGY—A plan or method for succeeding.

SYNTHETIC—Made in a laboratory, not in nature.

TRADITION—A belief or custom that is handed down from generation to generation.

TRAILED—Was behind.

UNPREDICTABLE—Difficult to predict or control.

WITNESSING—Being in a place to see what is going on.

Places to Go

ON THE ROAD

YANKEE STADIUM
161st Street and River Avenue
Bronx, NY 10451
(718) 293-4300

**NATIONAL BASEBALL
HALL OF FAME AND MUSEUM**
25 Main Street
Cooperstown, New York 13326
(888) 425-5633
www.baseballhalloffame.org

ON THE WEB

THE NEW YORK YANKEES
• *to learn more about the Yankees*
www.Yankees.com

MAJOR LEAGUE BASEBALL
• *to learn about all the major league teams*
www.mlb.com

MINOR LEAGUE BASEBALL
• *to learn more about the minor league system*
www.minorleaguebaseball.com

ON THE BOOKSHELVES

To learn more about the sport of baseball, look for these books at your library or bookstore:

• January, Brendan. *A Baseball All-Star*. Chicago, IL.: Heinemann Library, 2005.

• Kelly, James. *Baseball*. New York, NY.: DK, 2005.

• Mintzer, Rich. *The Everything Kids' Baseball Book*. Cincinnati, OH.: Adams Media Corporation, 2004.

Index

PAGE NUMBERS IN **BOLD** REFER TO ILLUSTRATIONS.

The Team

MARK STEWART has written more than 25 books on baseball, and over 100 sports books for kids. He grew up in New York City during the 1960s rooting for the Yankees and Mets, and now takes his two daughters, Mariah and Rachel, to the same ballparks. Mark comes from a family of writers. His grandfather was Sunday Editor of *The New York Times* and his mother was Articles Editor of *Ladies Home Journal* and *McCall's*. Mark has profiled hundreds of athletes over the last 20 years. He has also written several books about his native New York and New Jersey, his home today. Mark is a graduate of Duke University, with a degree in history. He lives with his daughters and wife, Sarah, overlooking Sandy Hook, NJ.

JAMES L. GATES, JR. has served as Library Director at the National Baseball Hall of Fame since 1995. He had previously served in academic libraries for almost fifteen years. He holds degrees from Belmont Abbey College, the University of Notre Dame and Indiana University. During his career Jim has authored several academic articles and has served in an editorial capacity on multiple book, magazine and museum publications, and he also serves as host for the Annual Cooperstown Symposium on Baseball and American Culture. He is an ardent Baltimore Orioles fan and enjoys watching baseball with his wife and two children.